I0469374

Praise

FAMOUS PSALMS & VERSES

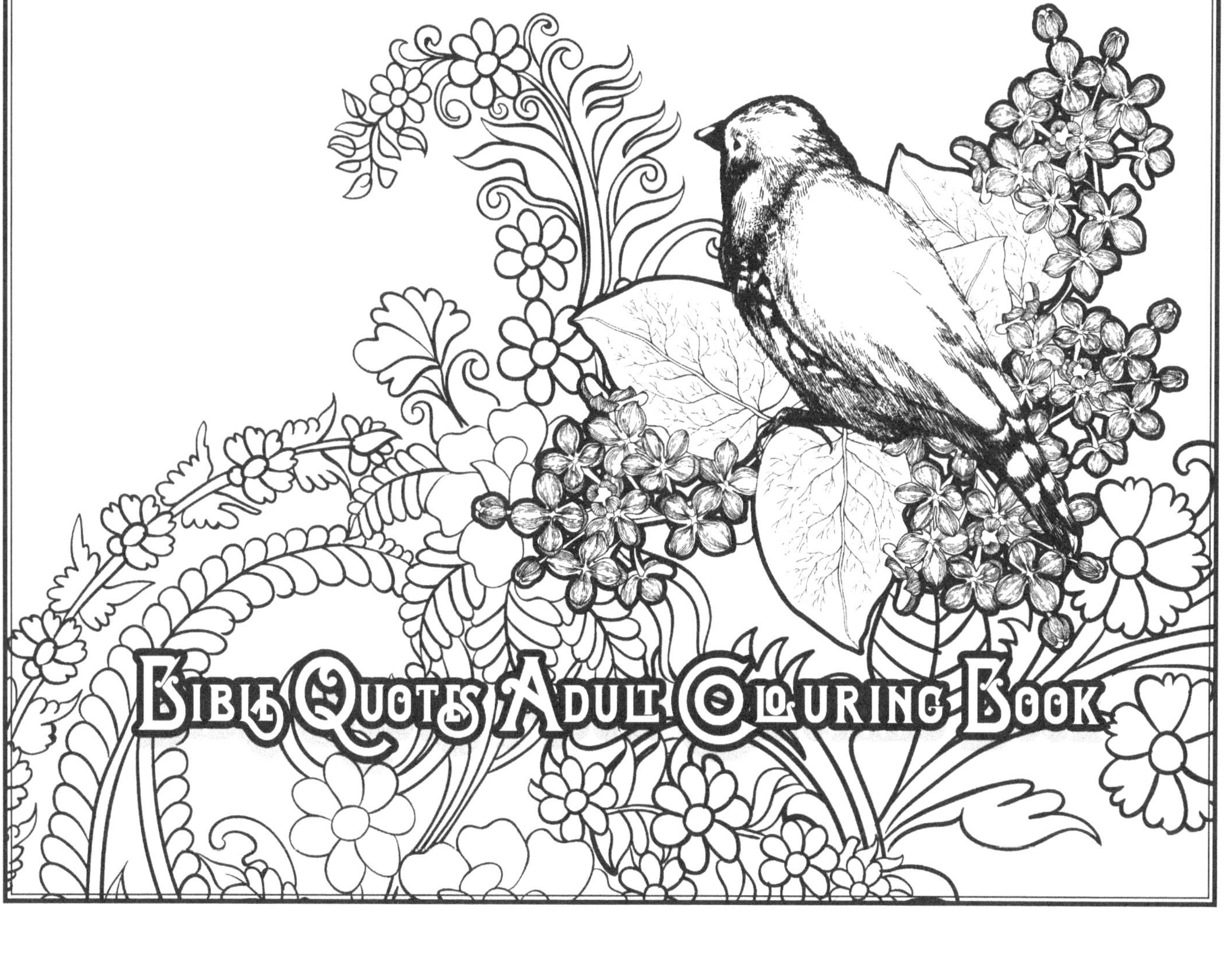

Bible Quotes Adult Colouring Book

Copyrights © 2016 All rights reserved
by: Bible Coloring Book
Drawn By Artists:
    Joshua Lazana Lagman and Jade Villaremo
    Mandala & Caricature Illustration
Art Director: lluontheloose

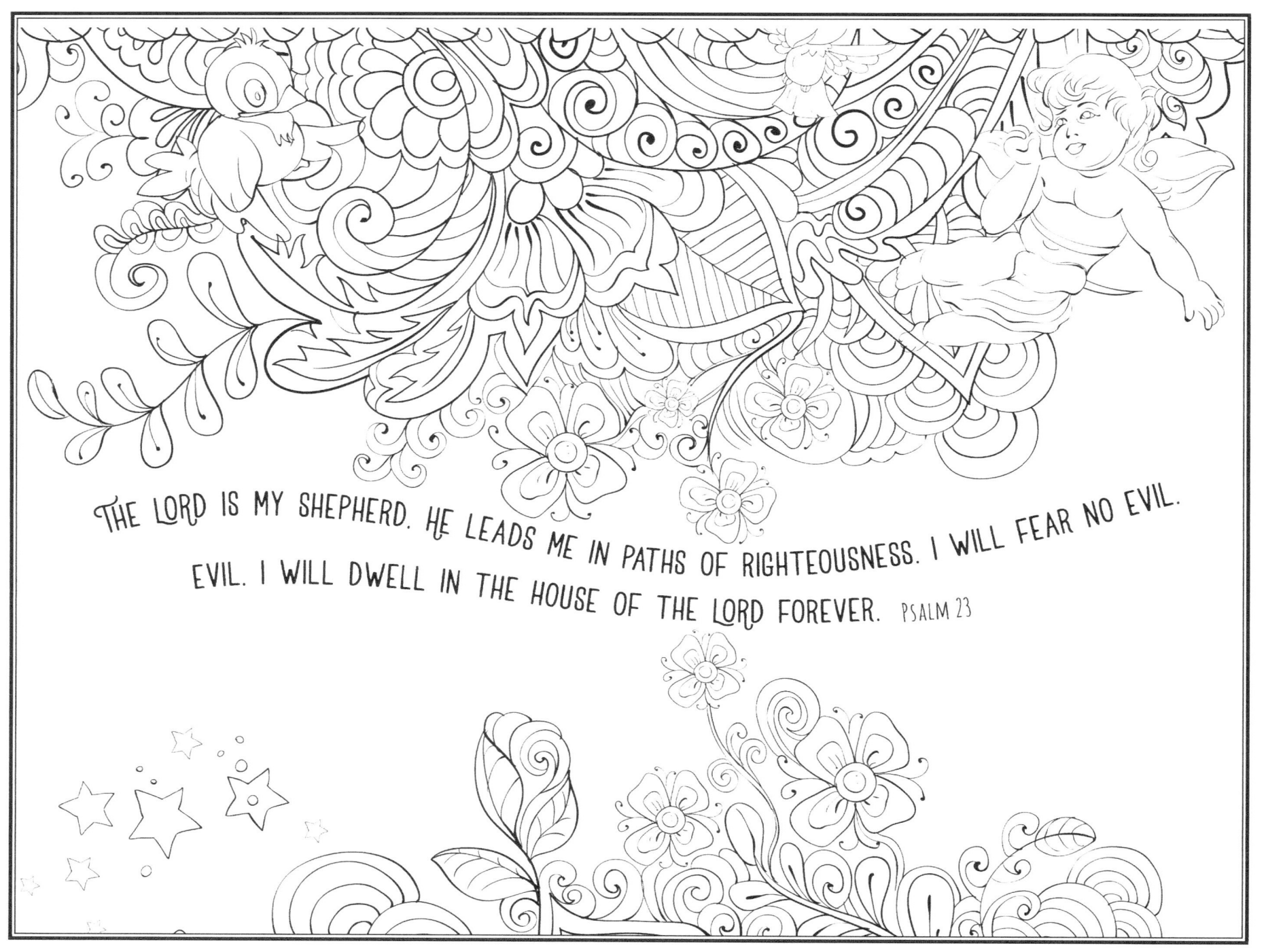

THE LORD IS MY SHEPHERD. HE LEADS ME IN PATHS OF RIGHTEOUSNESS. I WILL FEAR NO EVIL. EVIL. I WILL DWELL IN THE HOUSE OF THE LORD FOREVER. PSALM 23

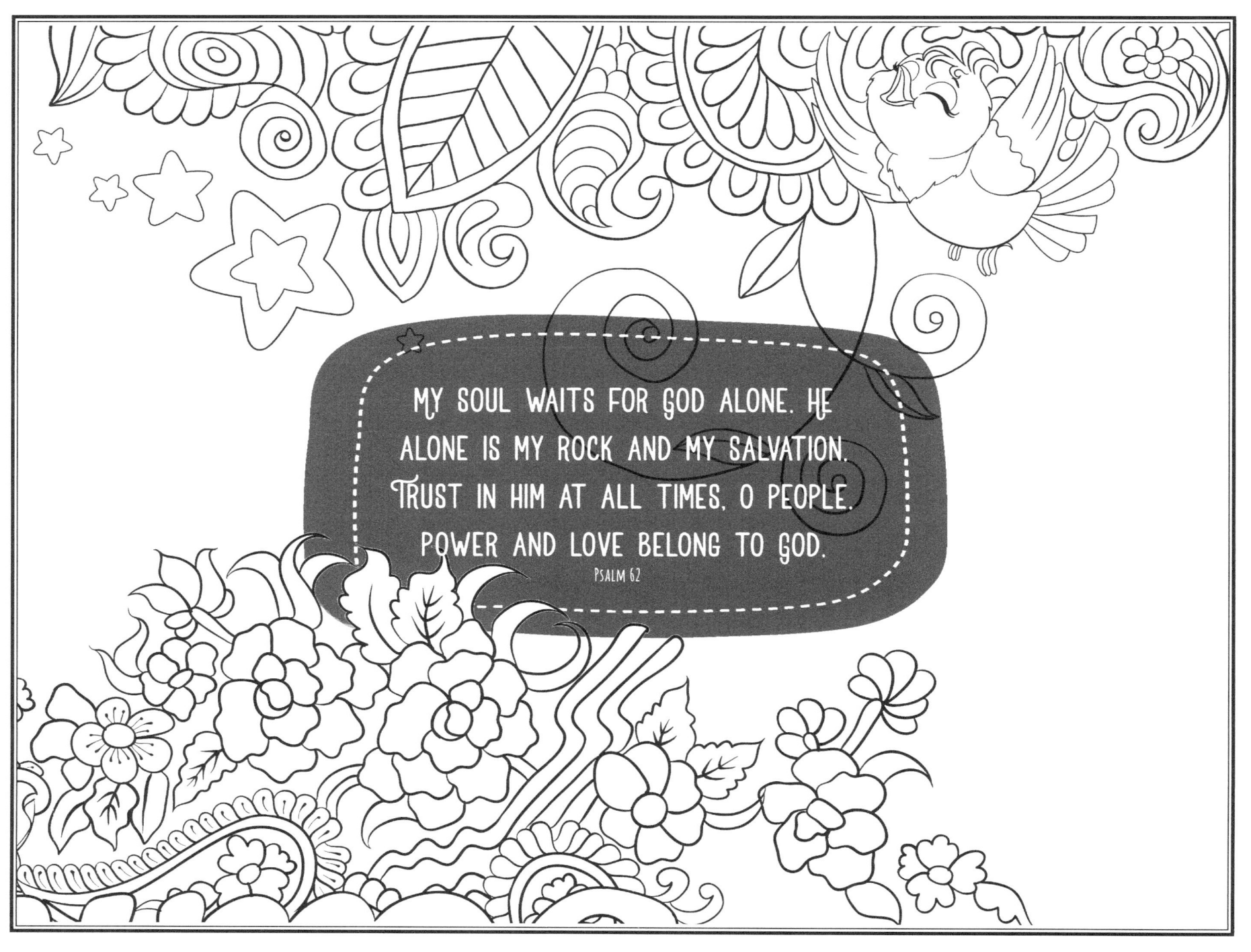

6

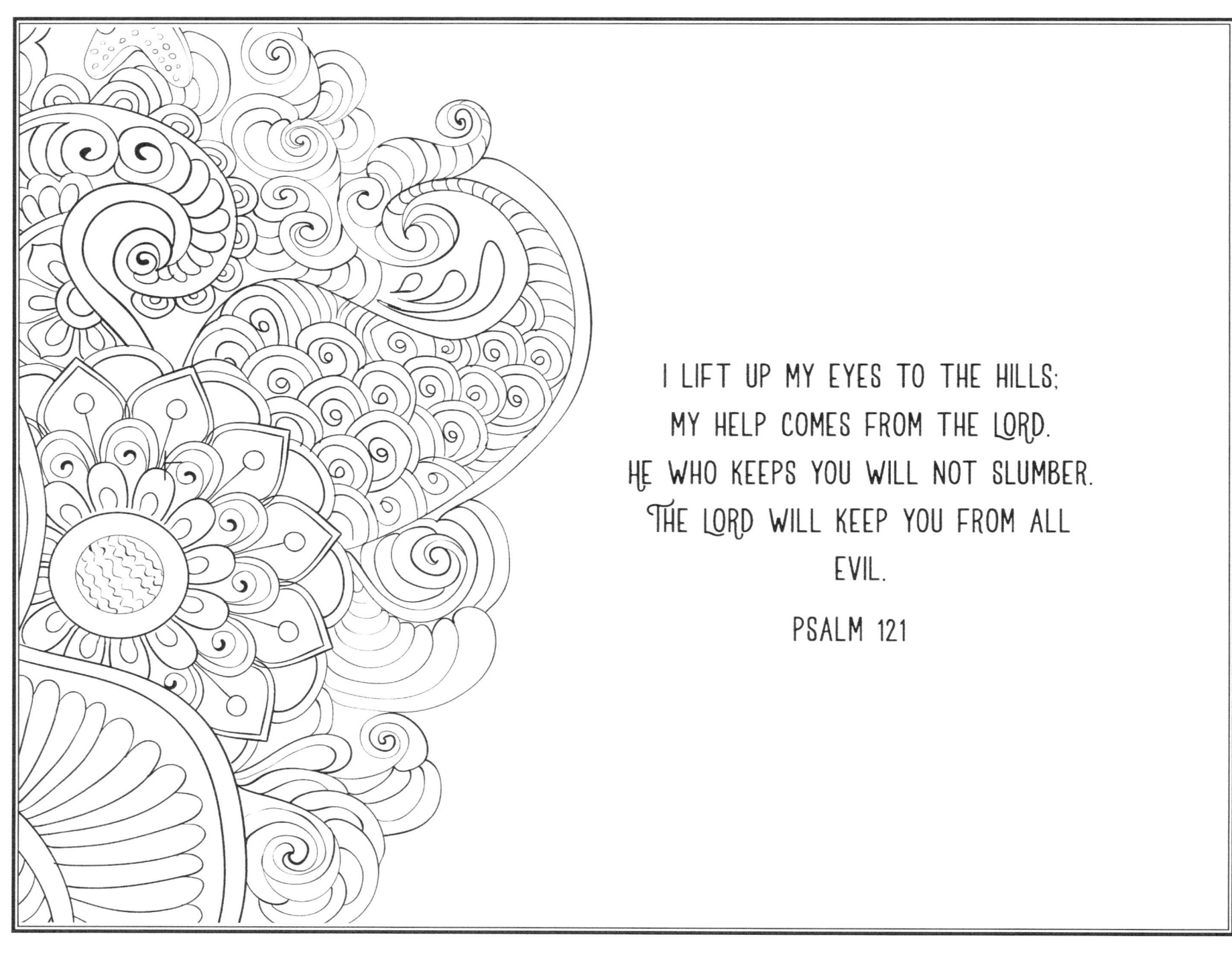

I LIFT UP MY EYES TO THE HILLS;
MY HELP COMES FROM THE LORD.
HE WHO KEEPS YOU WILL NOT SLUMBER.
THE LORD WILL KEEP YOU FROM ALL
EVIL.

PSALM 121

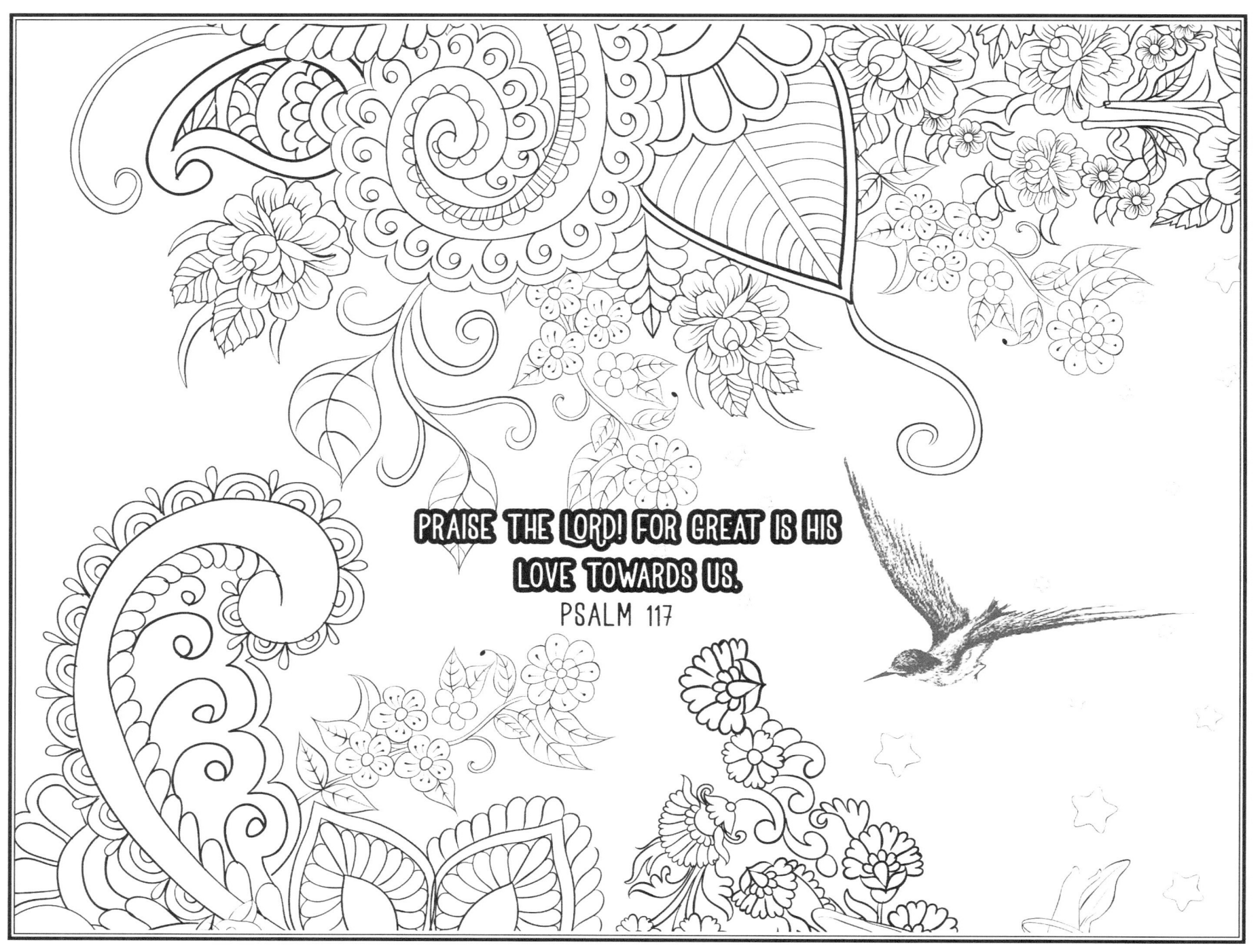

PRAISE THE LORD! FOR GREAT IS HIS LOVE TOWARDS US.

PSALM 117

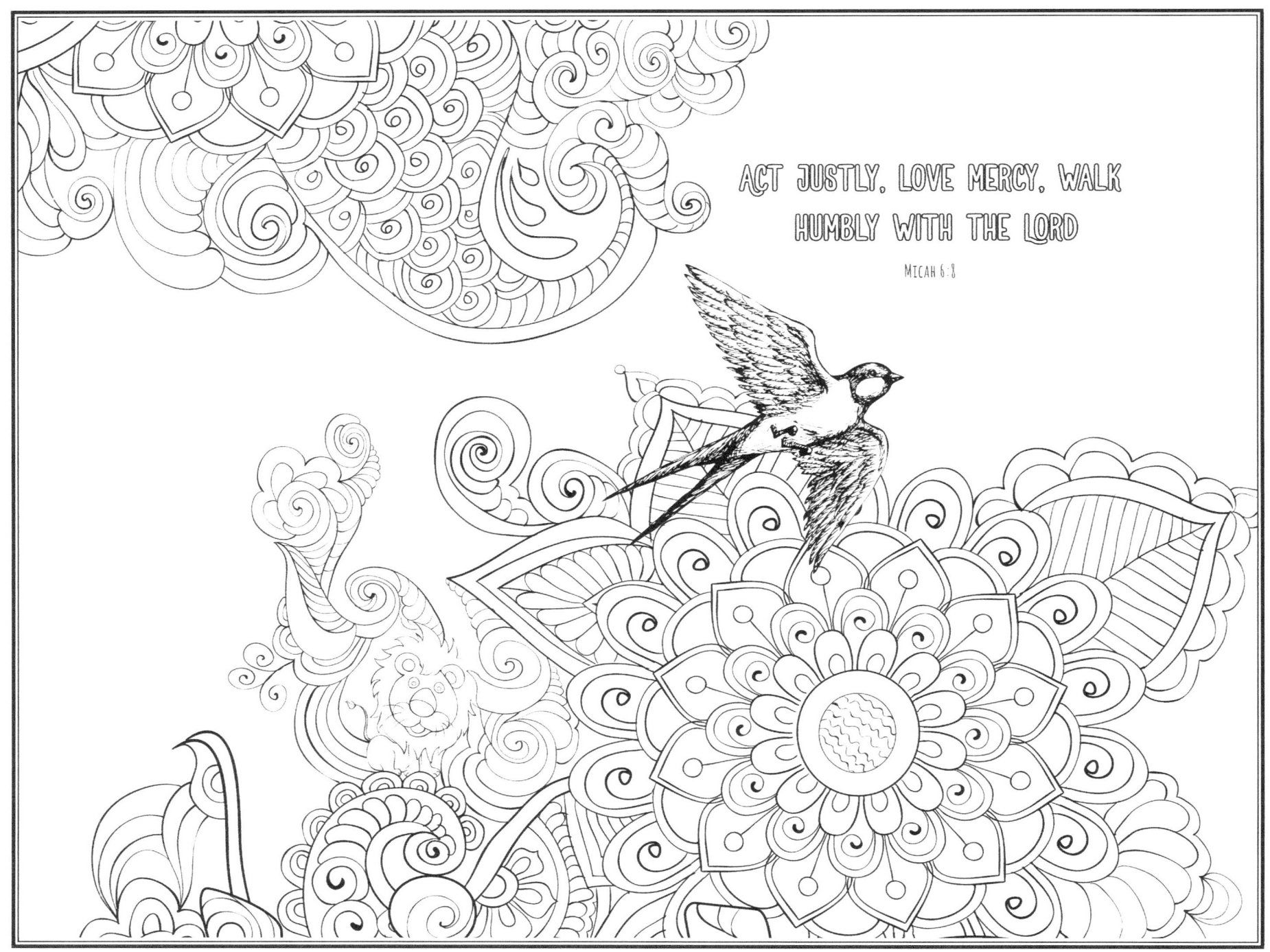

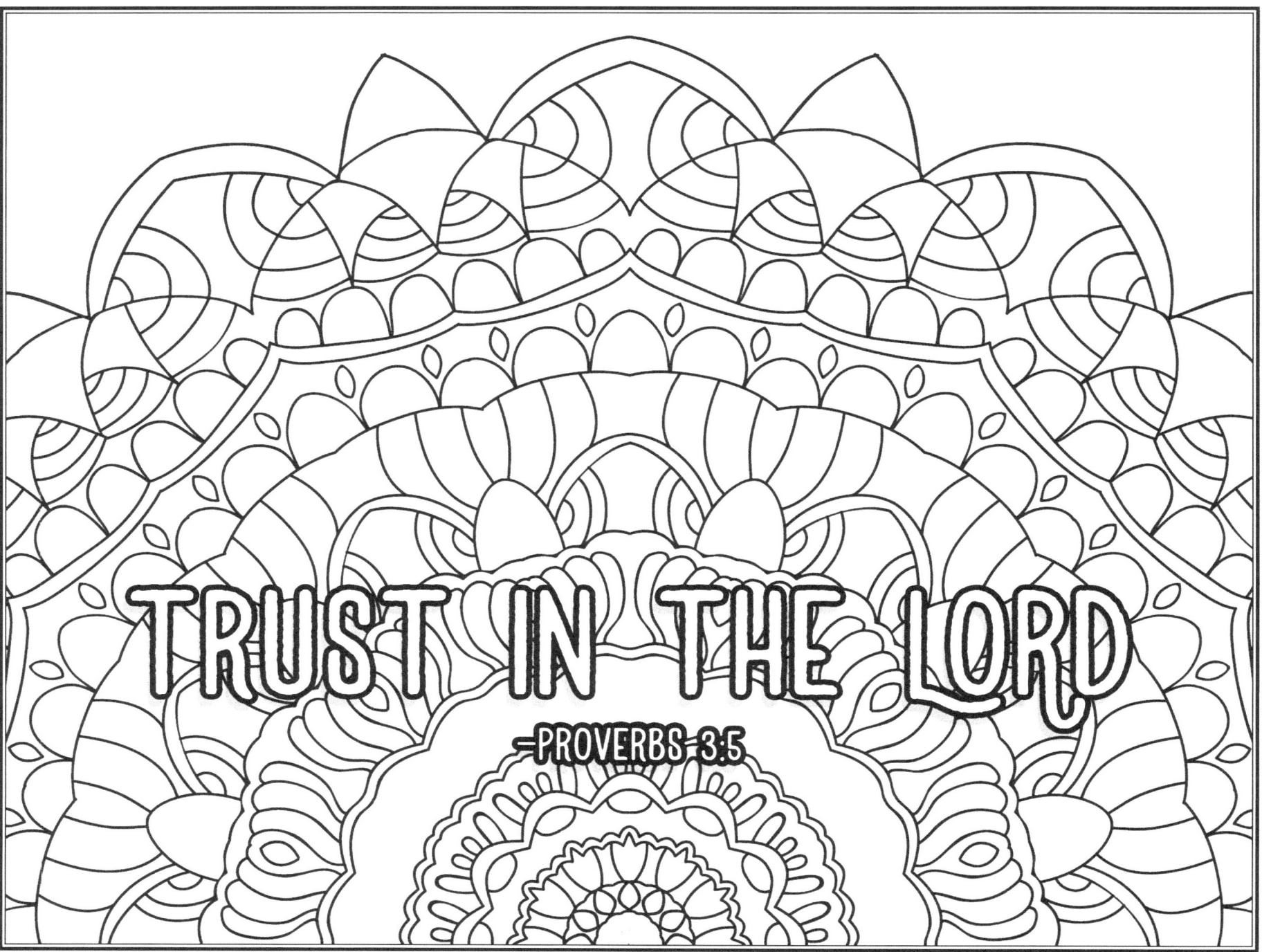

14

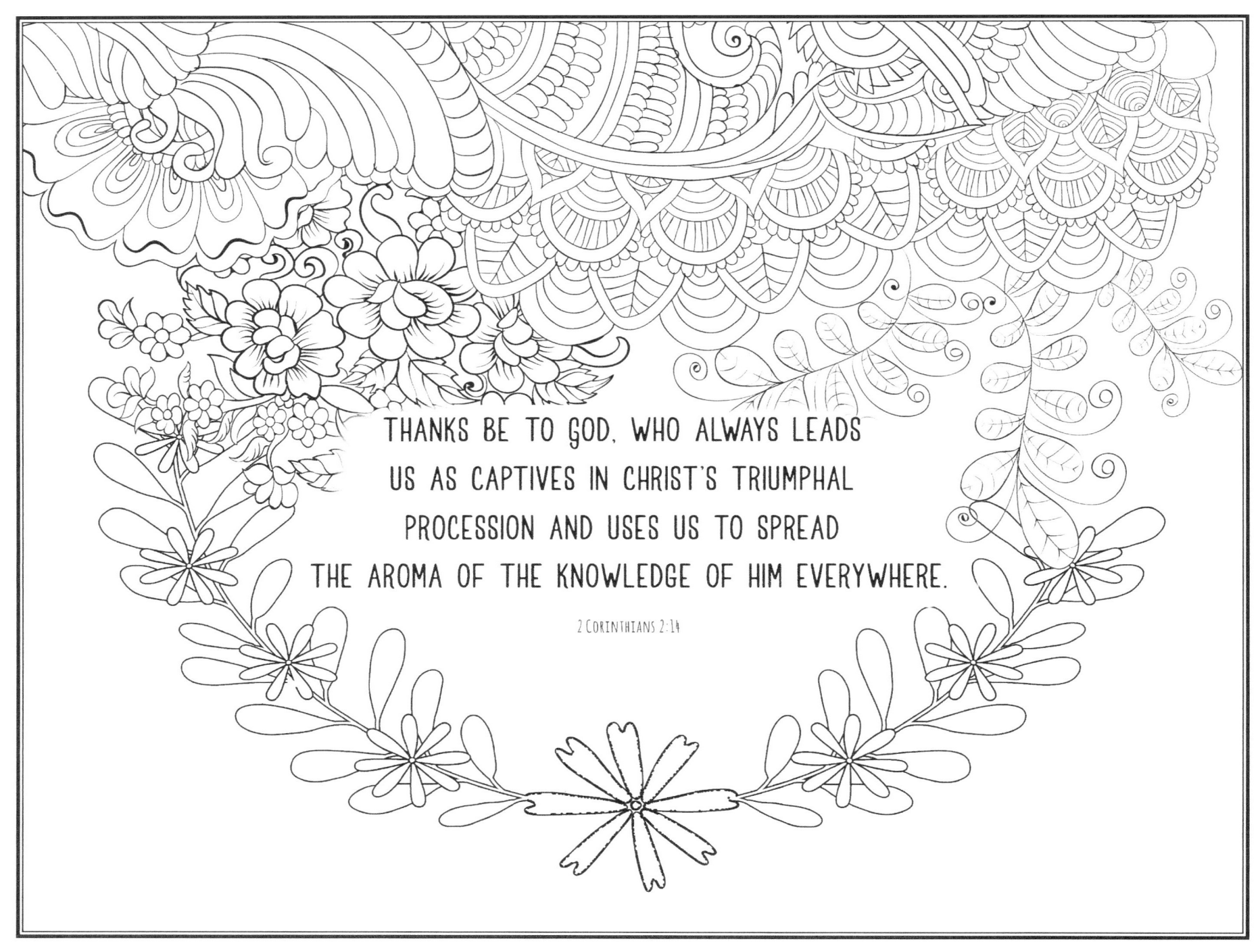

THANKS BE TO GOD, WHO ALWAYS LEADS
US AS CAPTIVES IN CHRIST'S TRIUMPHAL
PROCESSION AND USES US TO SPREAD
THE AROMA OF THE KNOWLEDGE OF HIM EVERYWHERE.

2 Corinthians 2:14

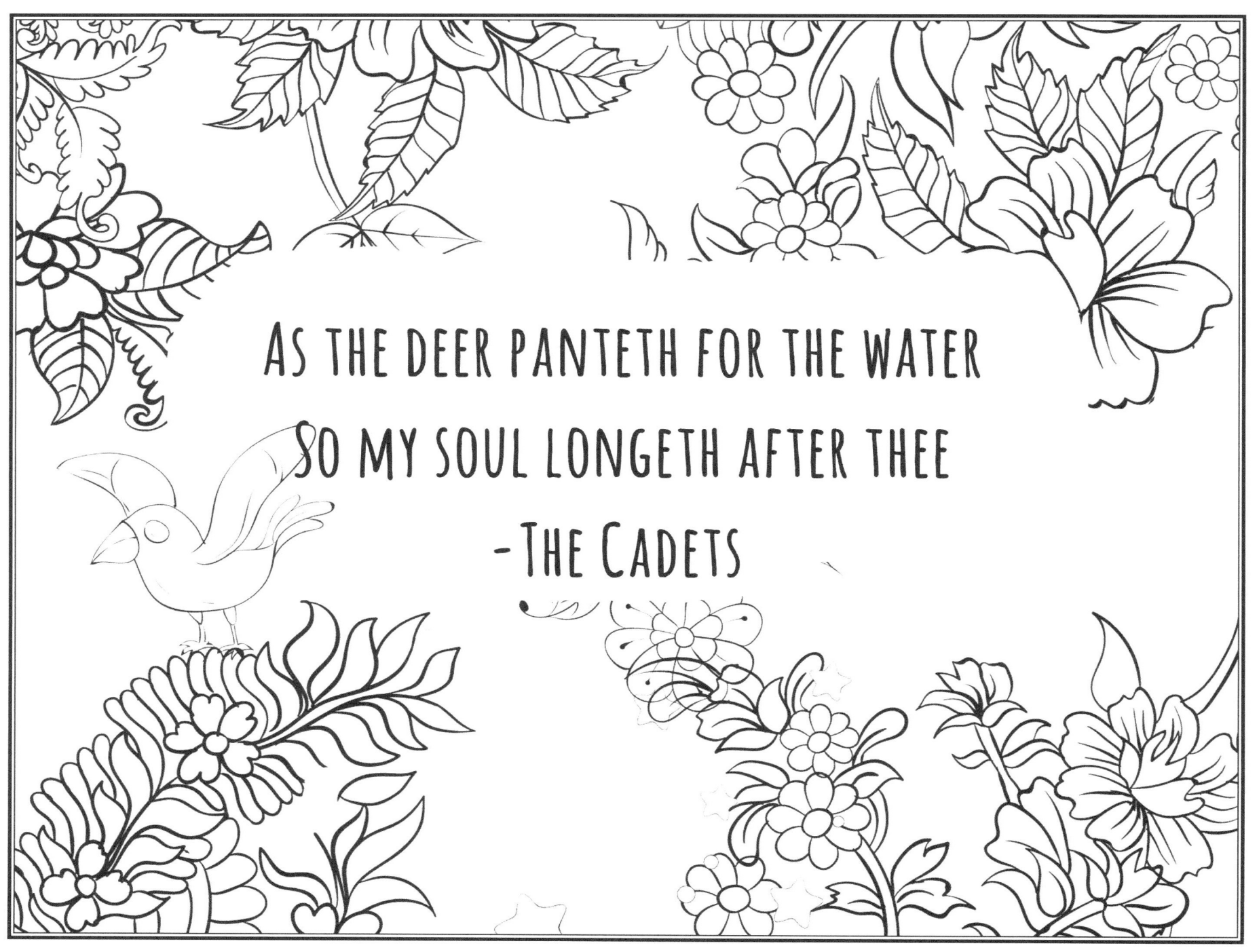

As the deer panteth for the water

So my soul longeth after thee

-The Cadets

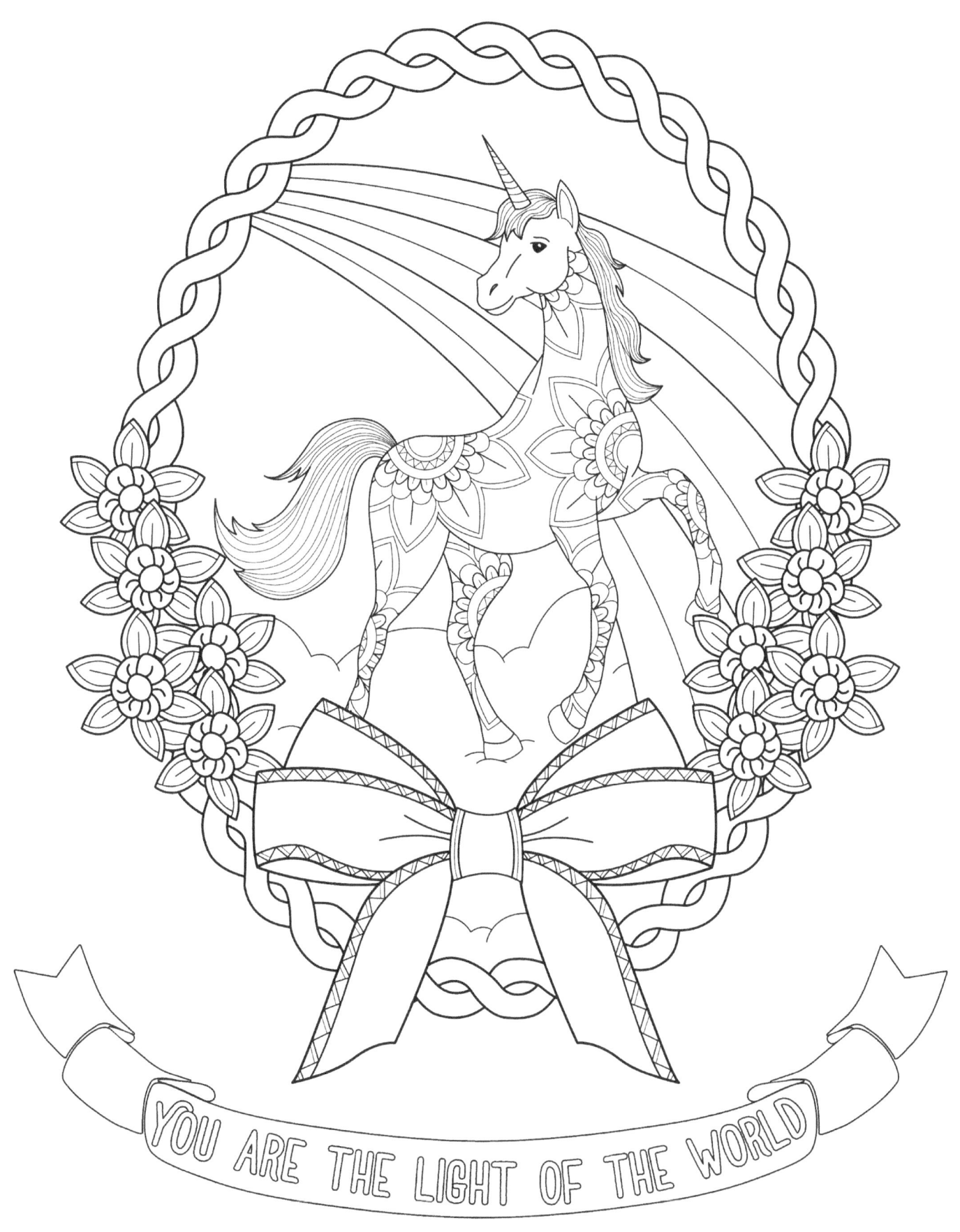

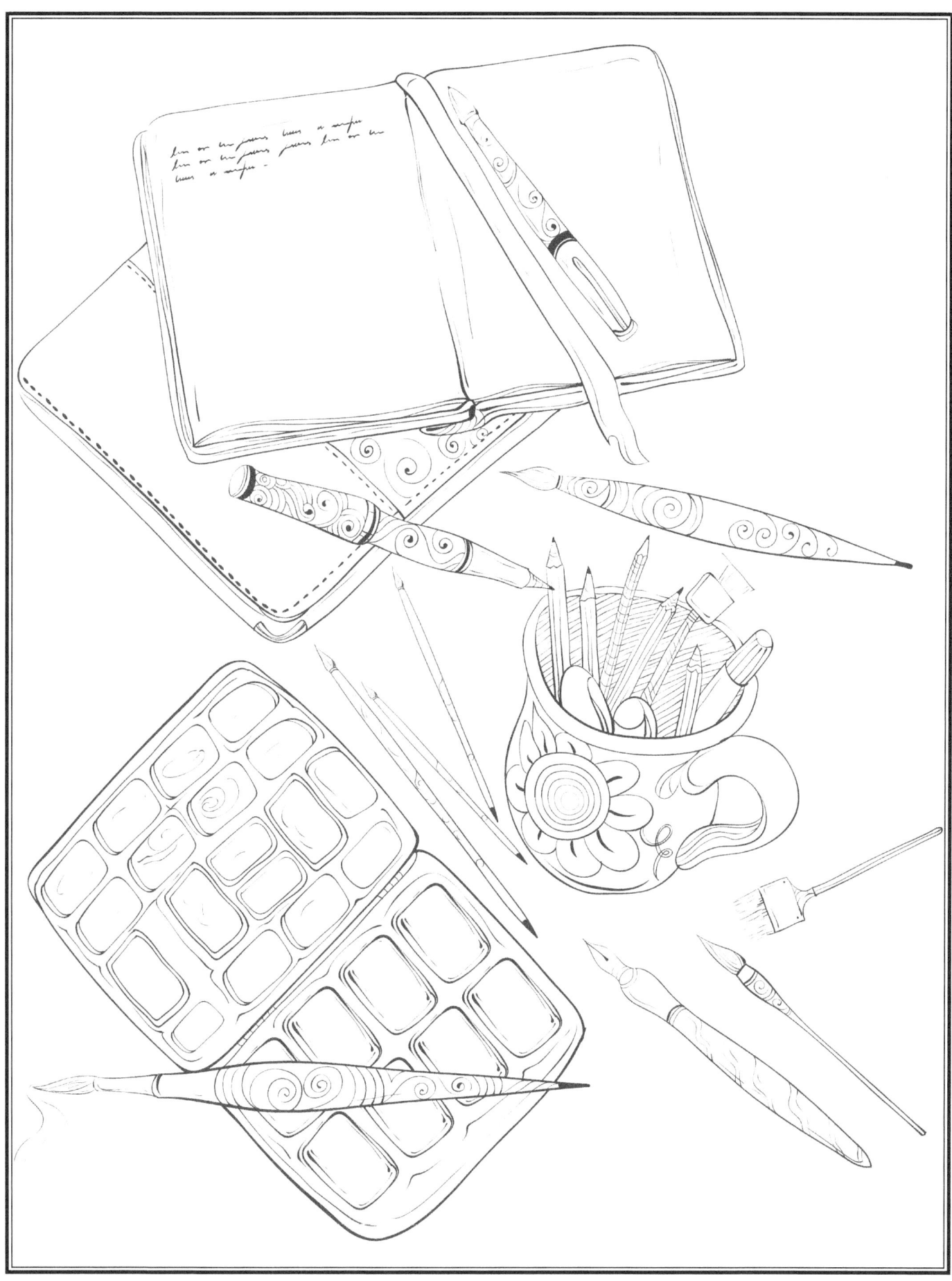

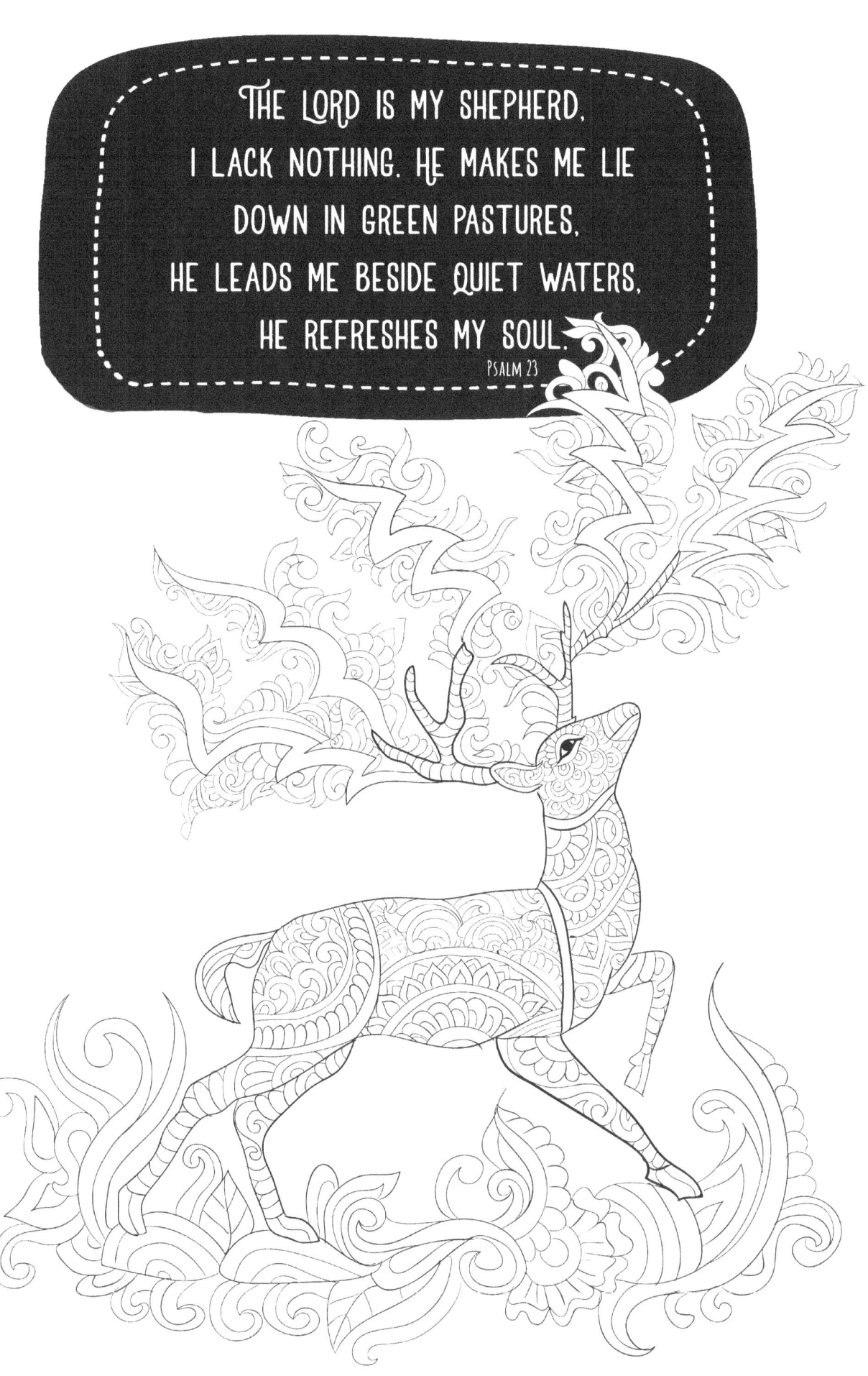

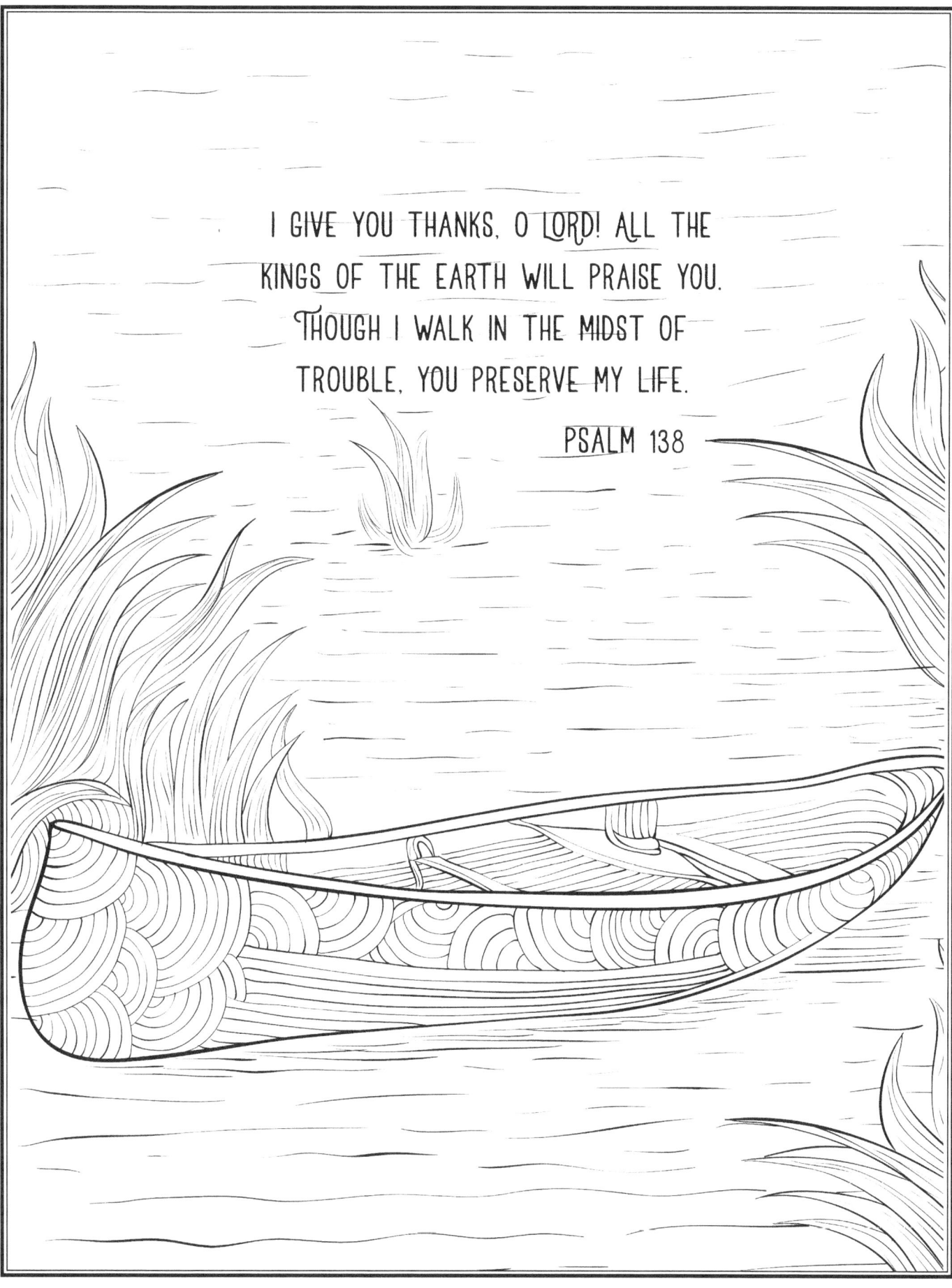

I GIVE YOU THANKS, O LORD! ALL THE KINGS OF THE EARTH WILL PRAISE YOU. THOUGH I WALK IN THE MIDST OF TROUBLE, YOU PRESERVE MY LIFE.

PSALM 138

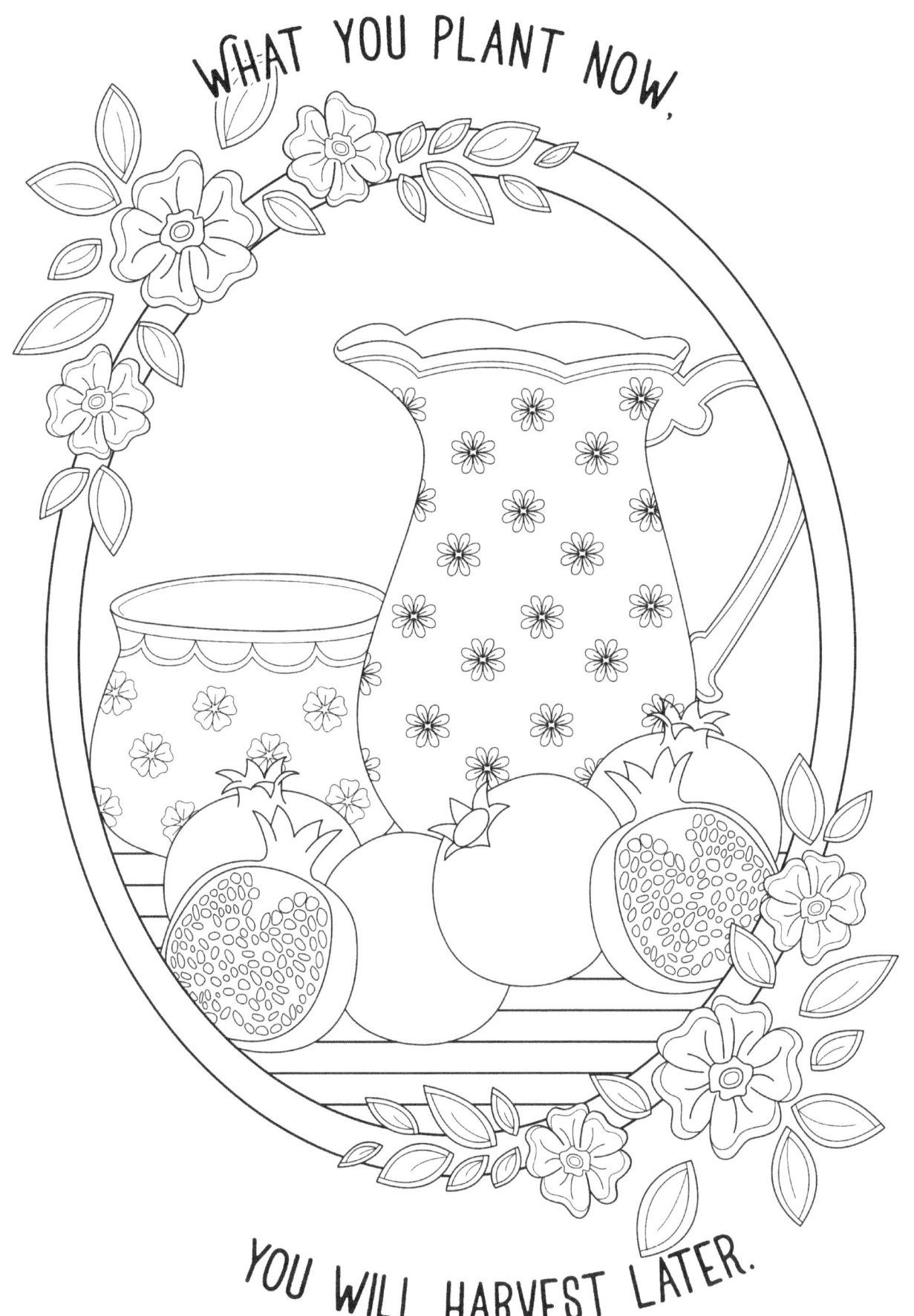

WHAT YOU PLANT NOW,

YOU WILL HARVEST LATER.

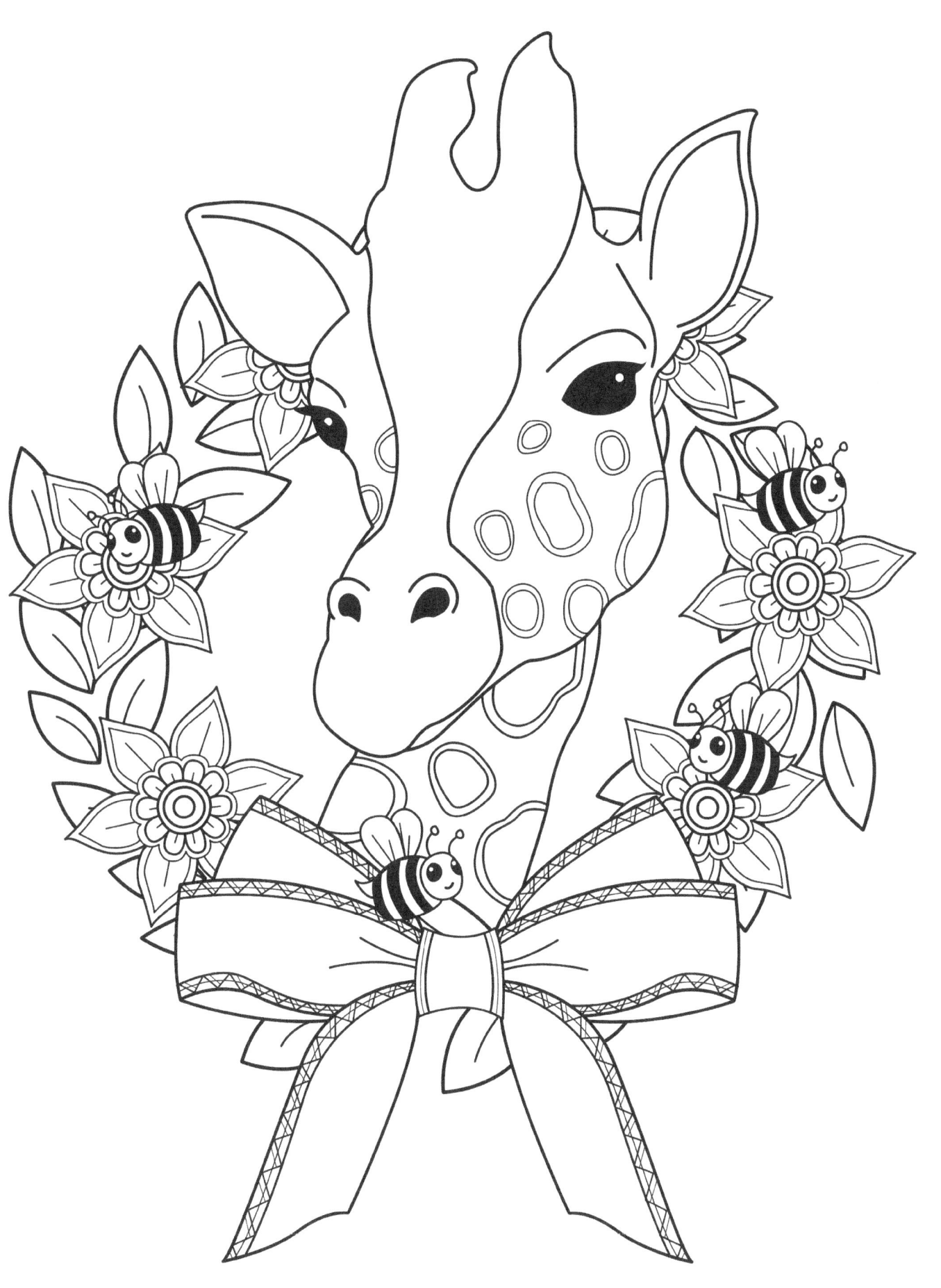

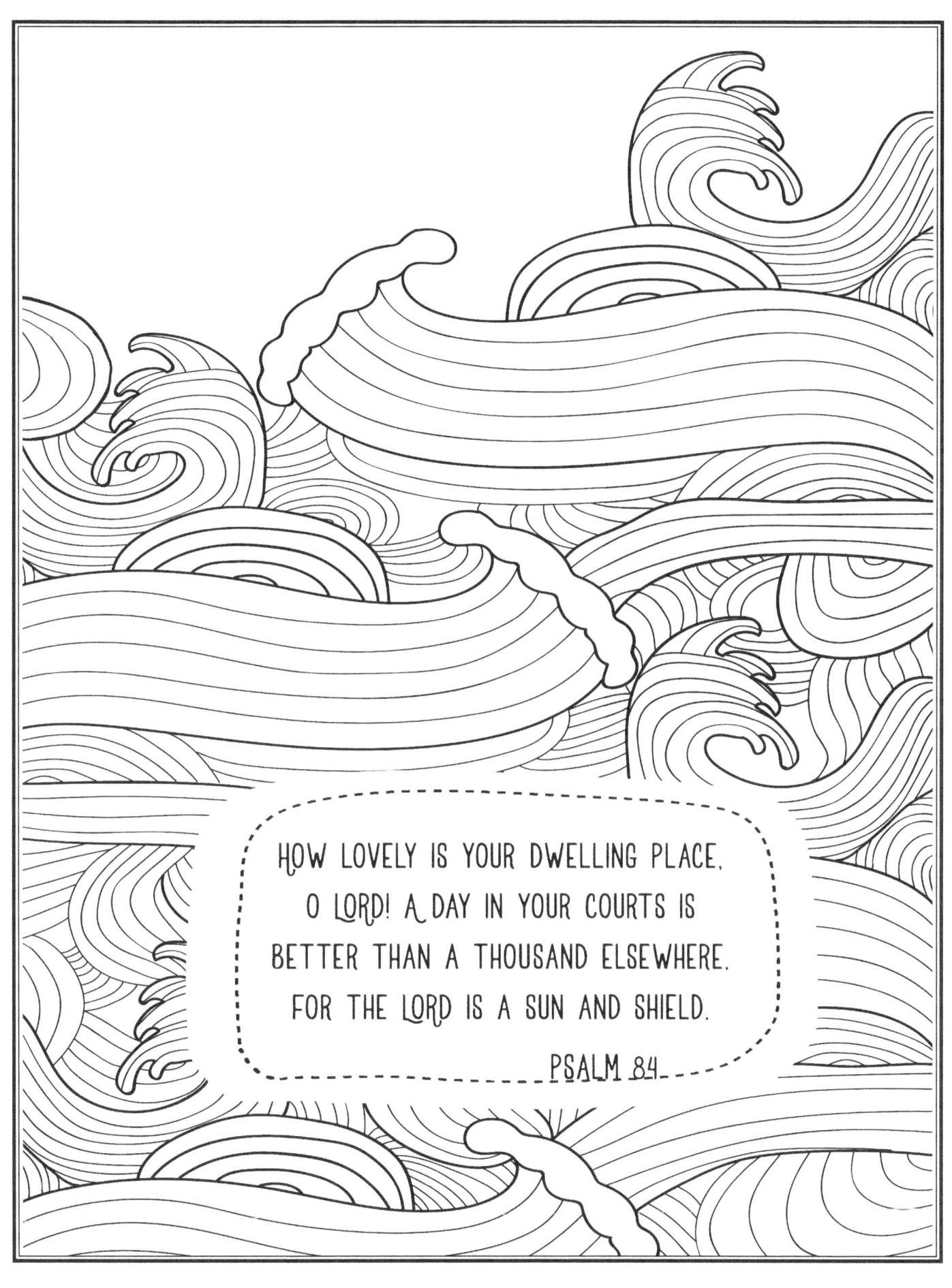

HOW LOVELY IS YOUR DWELLING PLACE,
O LORD! A DAY IN YOUR COURTS IS
BETTER THAN A THOUSAND ELSEWHERE.
FOR THE LORD IS A SUN AND SHIELD.

PSALM 84

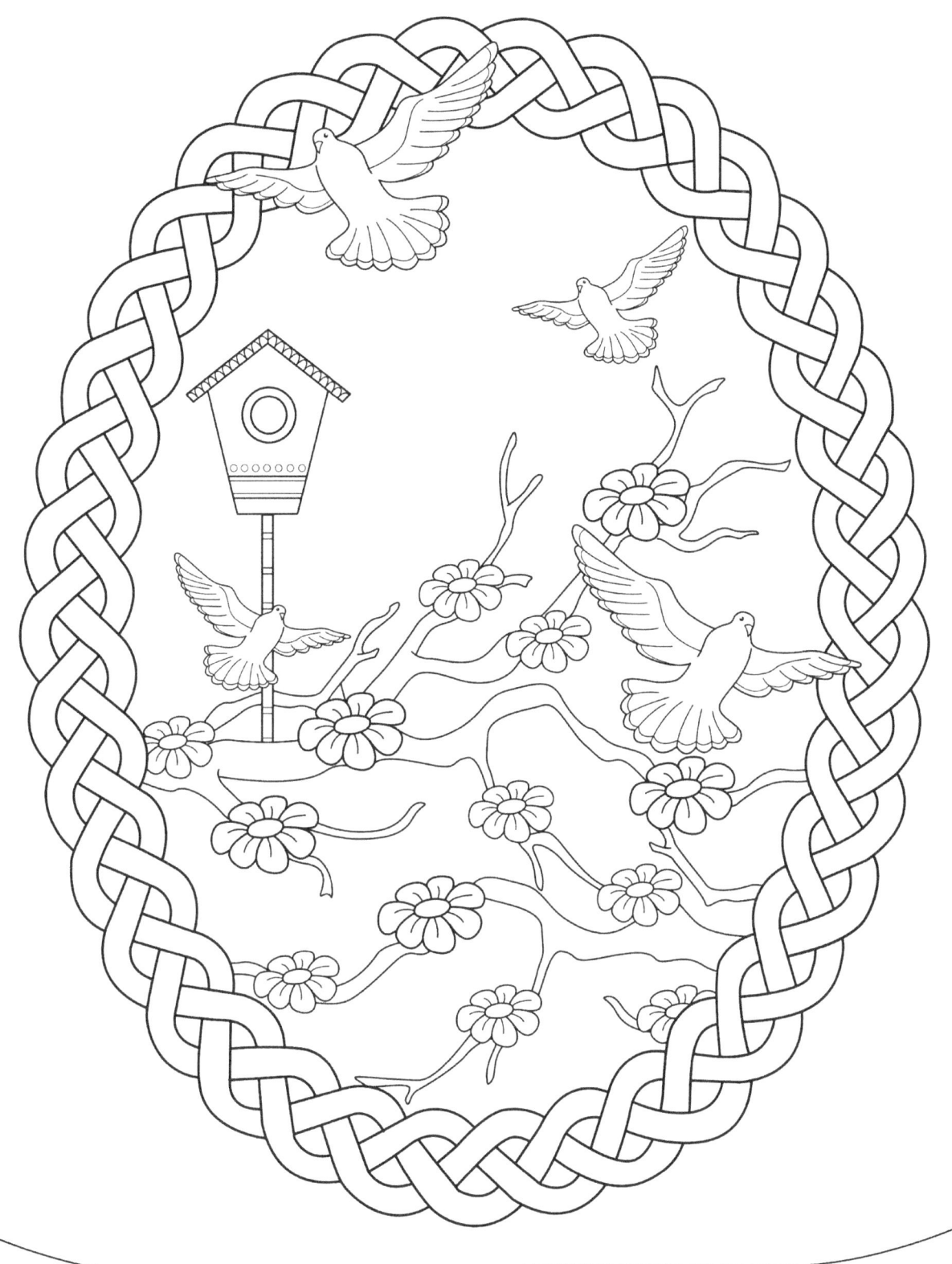

IF IT DOESN'T CHALLENGE YOU, IT WON'TCHANGE YOU.

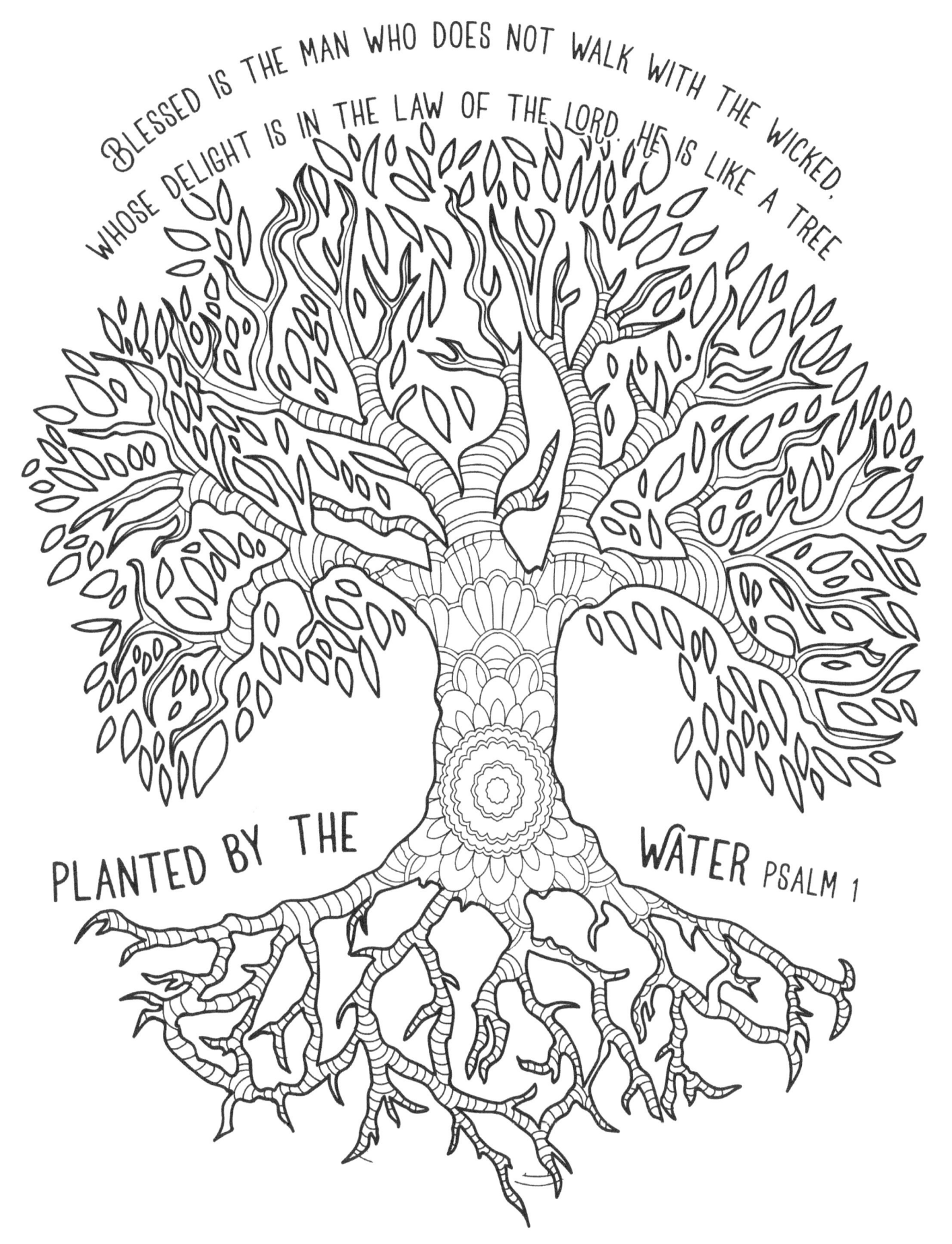

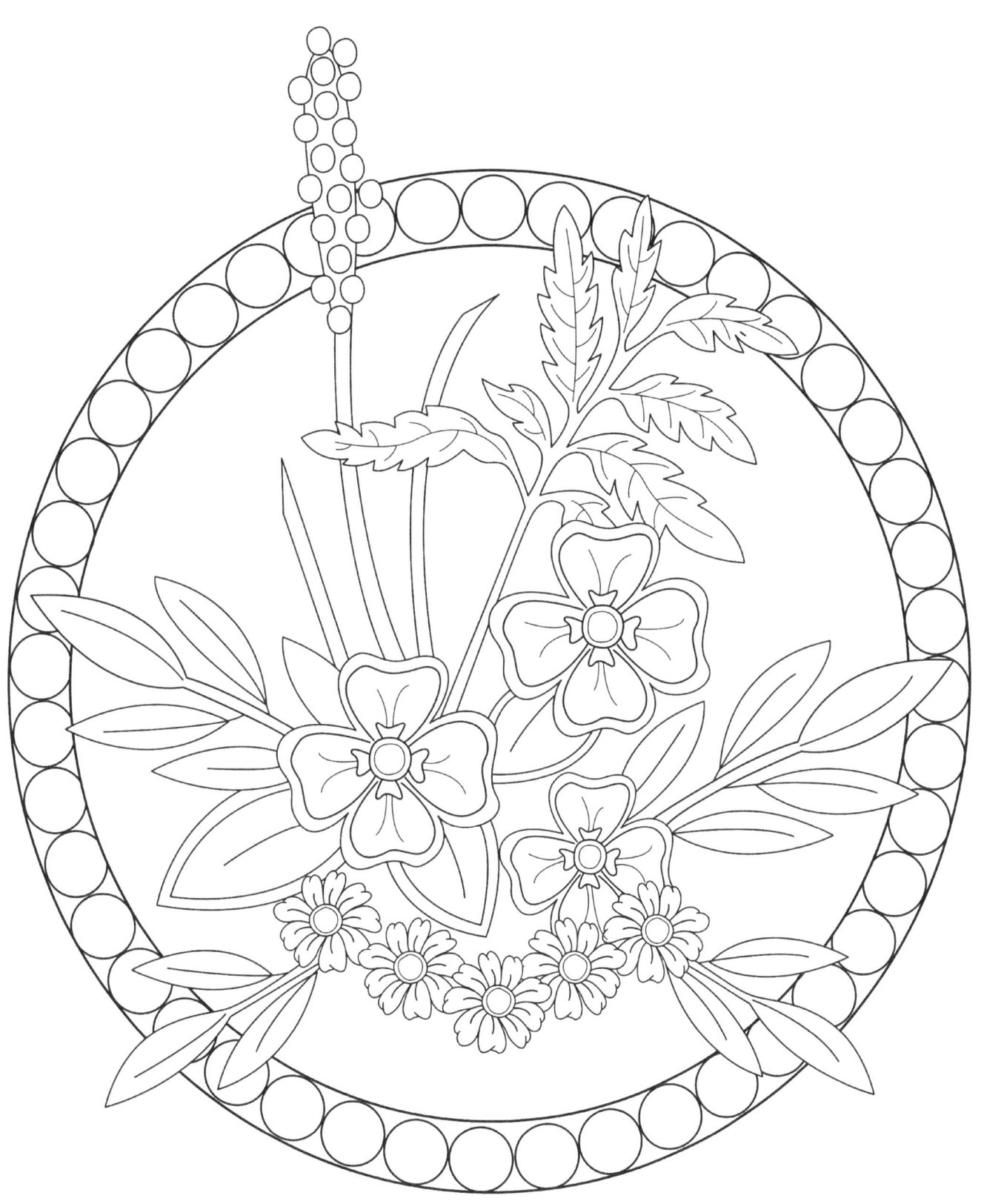

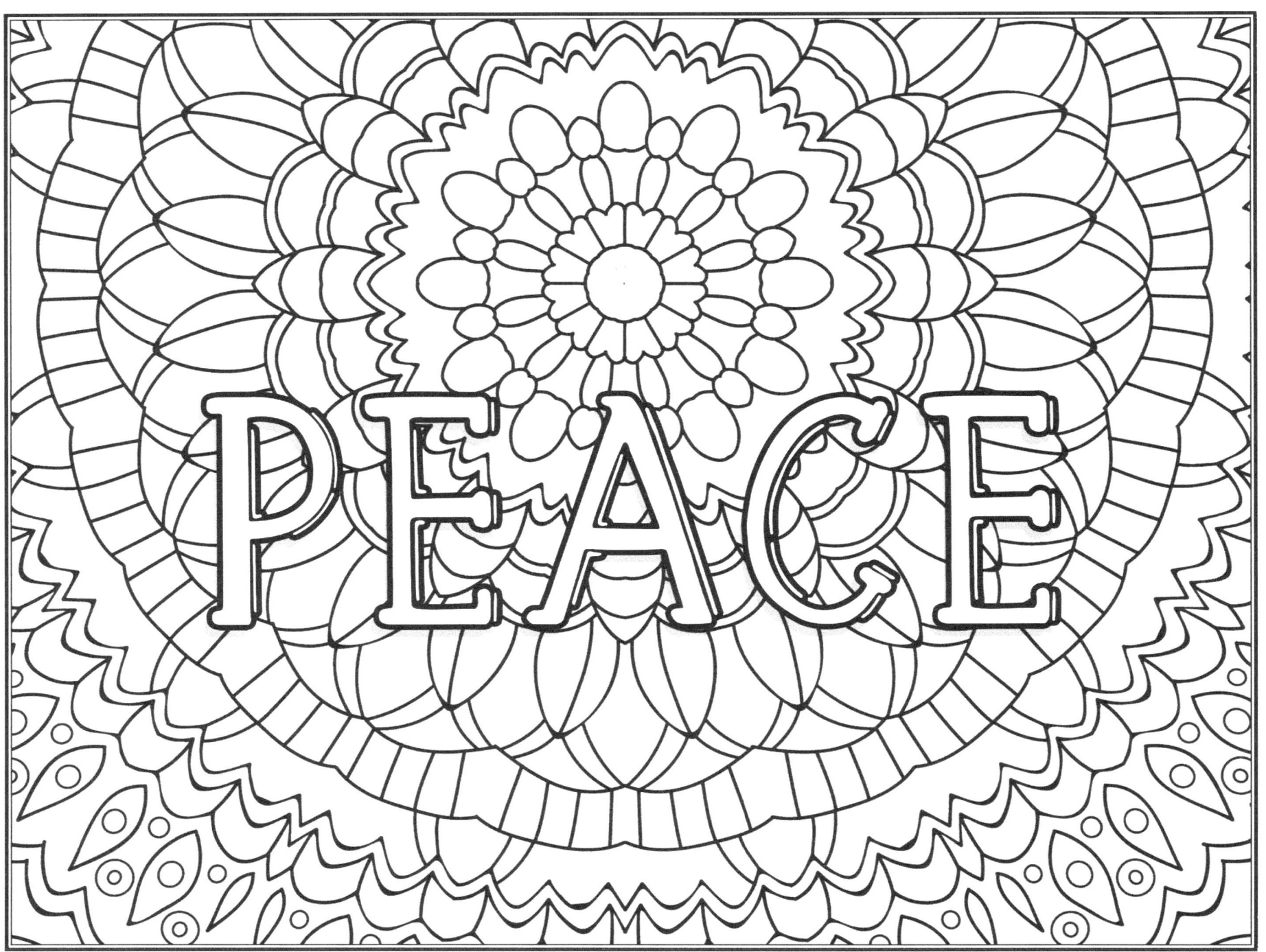

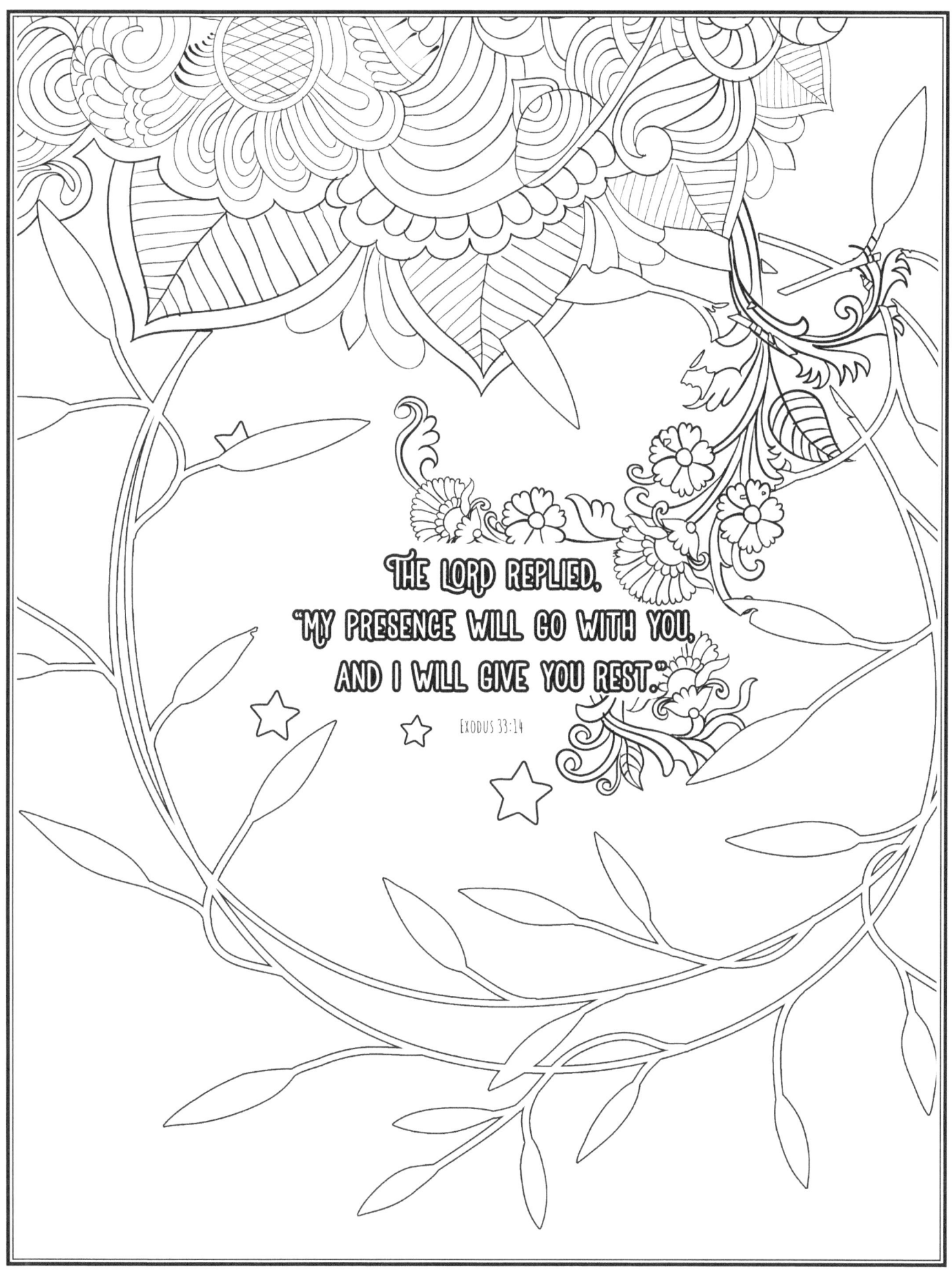

THE LORD REPLIED,
"MY PRESENCE WILL GO WITH YOU,
AND I WILL GIVE YOU REST."

Exodus 33:14

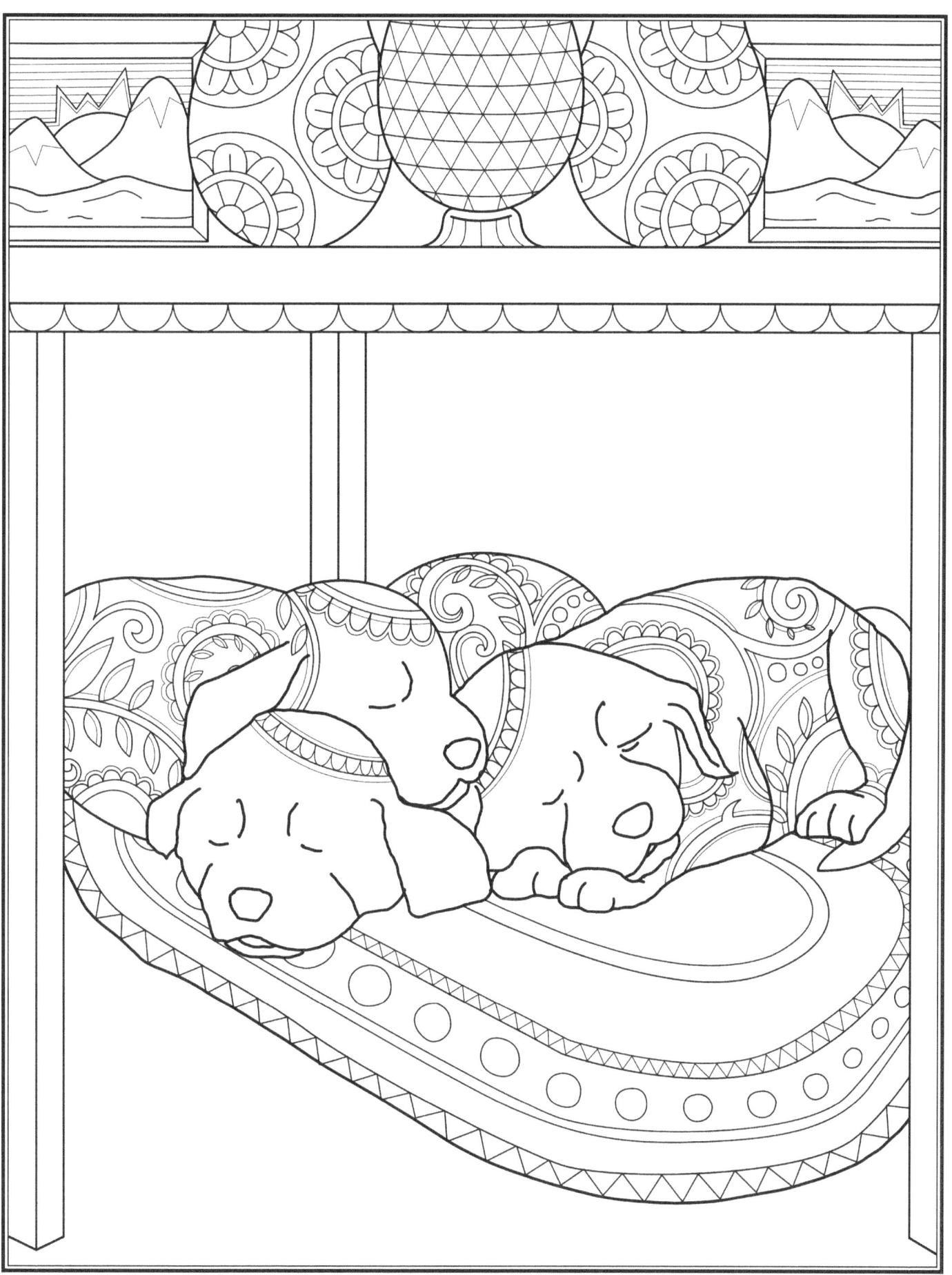

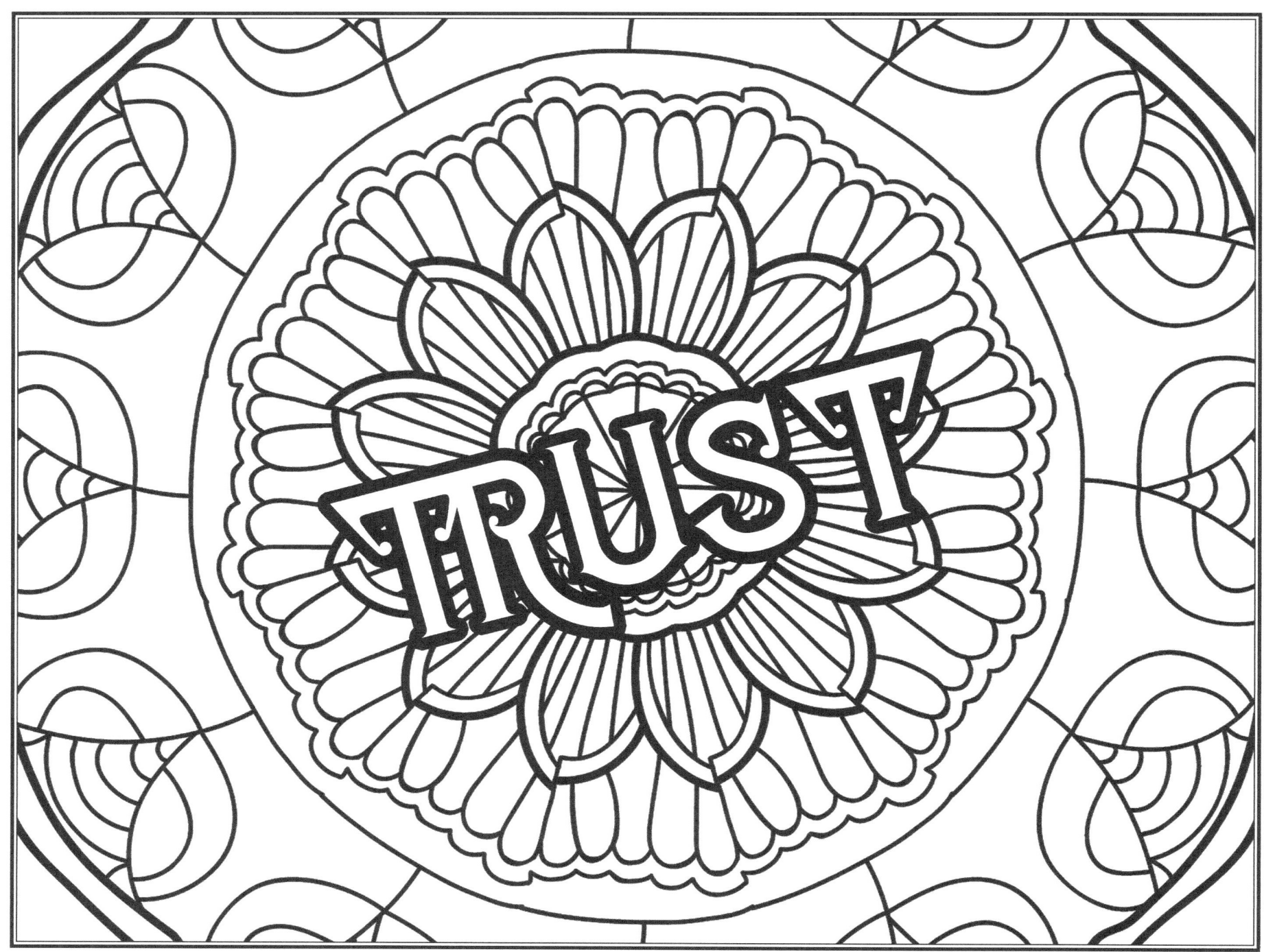

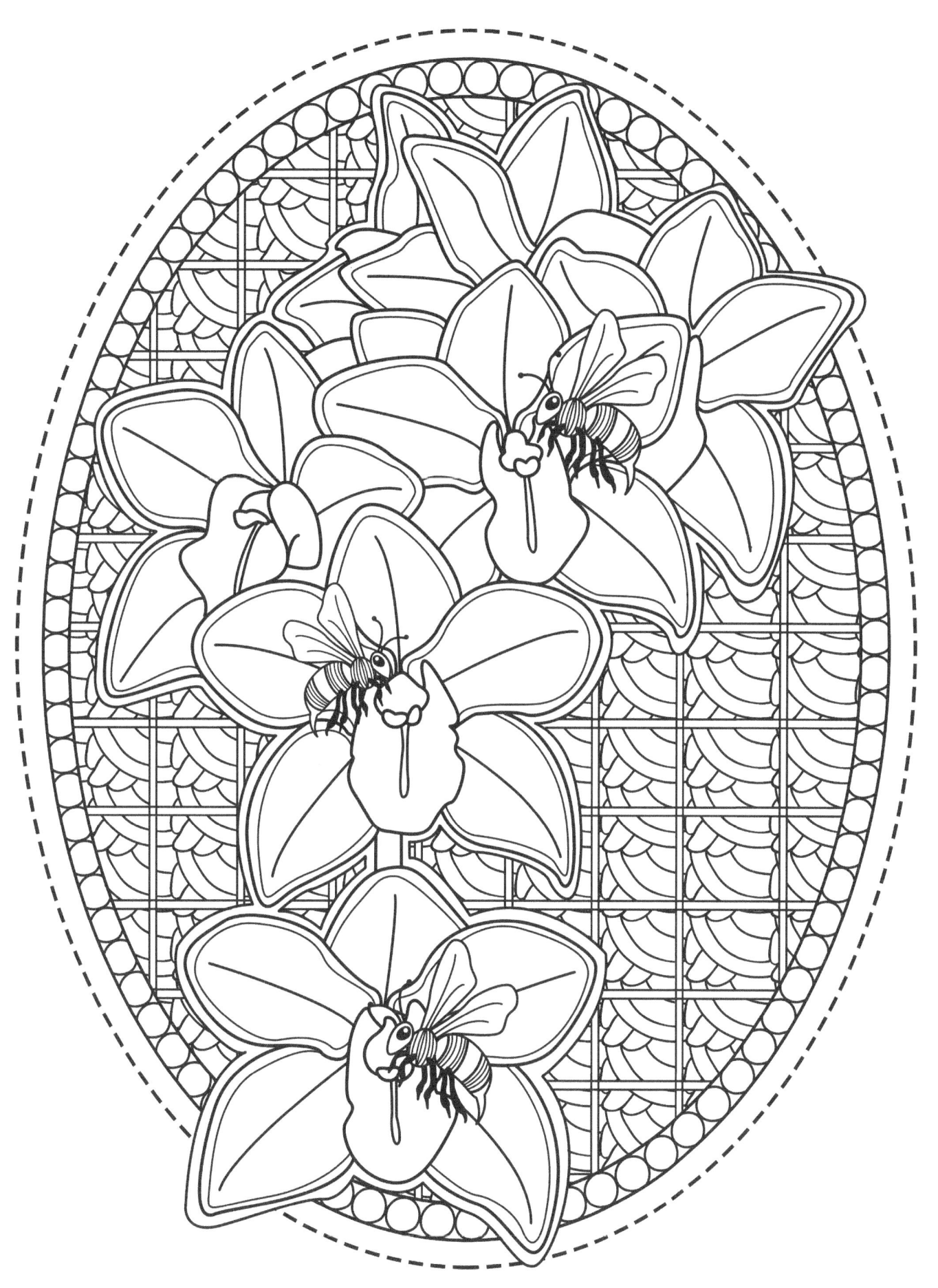

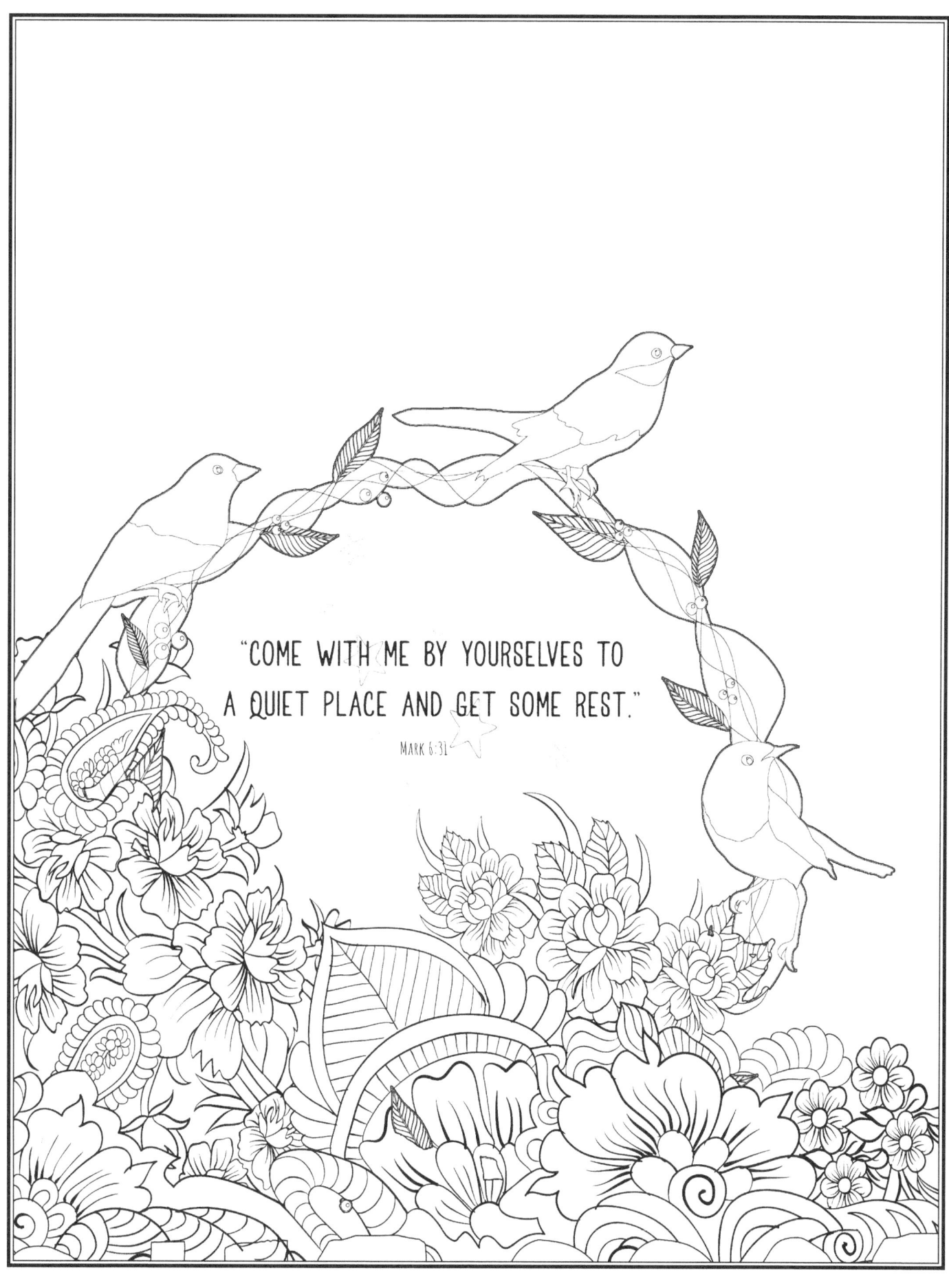

www.ingramcontent.com/pod-product-compliance
Lightning Source LLC
Chambersburg PA
CBHW080641190526
45169CB00009B/3448